Getting the Most for Your Health Care Dollar

A guide to health insurance and the Affordable Care Act

By Patricia D. King, J.D., M.B.A.

Copyright 2013 Digital Age Healthcare, LLC

Disclaimer: This document is intended as general information and does not constitute legal or tax advice. The information presented may not be applicable or appropriate for all individuals. Consult a licensed attorney or tax practitioner for legal or tax advice applicable to your situation.

Contents

Introduction	5
Insurance and health care costs: the big picture	5
The provider panel	6
Industry trends	7
1. The Affordable Care Act	**8**
1.1 What Is the Purpose of the Affordable Care Act?	8
1.2 Basics of the Affordable Care Act	10
1.2.1 The Health Insurance Reform Provisions of the ACA	11
1.2.2 Essential Health Benefits	14
1.2.3 Actuarial Values (Metal Levels)	15
1.2.4 Grandfathered Plans	16
1.2.5 Model Summary of Benefits	17
2. Health insurance exchanges	**18**
2.1 Who runs the exchange?	19
2.2 Who qualifies for coverage?	20
2.3 Who qualifies for subsidies?	21
2.3.1 Household Income in Relation to Federal Poverty Line	22
2.3.2 Enrollment in a Qualified Health Plan	22
2.3.3 Eligibility for Other Minimum Essential Coverage	22
2.4 How Much Are Premium Assistance Tax Credit Subsidies?	23
2.5 When Can You Enroll in a Plan Through the Exchange?	24
2.6 What Insurance Options Will You Find on the Exchange?	25
3. Health insurance basics	**27**
3.1 HMOs versus PPOs	27
3.2 Cost-Sharing	29
3.2.1 Deductibles	31
3.2.2 Coinsurance	31
3.2.3 Copayments	32
3.2.4 Ceiling on annual or lifetime benefits	33
3.2.5 Out-of-pocket maximums	33
3.2.6 Coverage Examples	33
3.3 Provider network	35
3.4 Covered benefits	36
3.4.1 Exclusions	37

3.5	Grievance procedures	38
3.6	Coordination of Benefits and Third Party Liability	38
4. Special tax benefits to pay health care costs		39
4.1	Flexible spending accounts	39
4.2	Health Savings Accounts	39
5. Health Insurance Through Your Employer		40
Conclusion		42
About the author		43

Introduction

The goal of this book is to help you get the most out of your health insurance coverage, whether you get coverage through your employer, through the health insurance exchanges created under the Affordable Care Act, or through a policy you purchase directly from the health insurance company. This is not a political or partisan book, nor does it go deep into the weeds of health policy. This book is solely devoted to you, the health care consumer. (So the book will be a useful reference to insurance brokers and other professionals, references to the federal regulations are included in many cases.)

The first two chapters will be most useful to anyone planning to get insurance coverage through the health care exchanges created under the Affordable Care Act. The remaining chapters apply to anyone with private health insurance, whether you get insurance through the exchange, through your employer, or directly from a health insurance company. (This book does not, however, address Medicaid or Medicare benefits.)

First, let's start with some background. Understanding the financial incentives acting on health insurance companies and health care providers can help you understand where they're coming from, and make the best choice for yourself. Insurance companies and health care providers, like anyone else, respond to economic incentives – and the economics of the health care industry are evolving rapidly.

Insurance and health care costs: the big picture

There are practically endless variations in health insurance arrangements, and it is not easy to know what options are best for you. When you are evaluating different insurance options, it's important to focus on the total cost to you, not just on the premium cost for the insurance itself. Health insurance always involves what the industry calls "cost sharing": deductibles, coinsurance and copayments. When an insurance company is designing a benefit plan, it uses cost sharing not only to cut the costs it has to pay, but also to give the consumer "skin in the game". The insurer expects that this will prompt the consumer to be more cost-conscious in deciding what health care services he/she needs, and help to control total costs by decreasing the volume of services.

The provider panel

The second factor to consider is the provider panel. This is also related to cost. You will often find that there are trade-offs between the cost of insurance, and your freedom to choose your health care provider. Why is there a trade-off between cost and freedom of choice? To put together its insurance offering, a health insurer has to decide not only on its plan design, but also its provider network. The provider network is composed of the primary care providers, specialists, hospitals and other health care entities that sign contracts with the insurer to be "participating providers" in the plan. There are a variety of financial arrangements used in these contracts, but generally speaking, the health insurer will get a better deal from a health care provider if the provider thinks that a lot of patients will be covered under the contract. So if the health insurer sets up a "narrow network", the patients covered by that insurer will be spread over a smaller number of providers, and the providers will likely contract with the plan on a favorable basis (e.g., a higher discount). Also, in a plan using a smaller network, the insurer may be better able to monitor the services provided. This is called "utilization review", and involves the procedures set up by the insurer to require pre-approval of certain high-cost services, to review the care provided to assure that it is "medically necessary", and to catch inappropriate billing practices.

What you will pay for health insurance also depends strongly on local market factors. Unlike markets for consumer goods, the cost of health care and health insurance can vary greatly from one area of the U.S. to another. This is influenced by the number of health insurers and health care providers competing in a particular market area, the relative market power of health insurers and health care providers, and even differences in practice patterns of physicians from one area to the next.

Industry trends

Finally, it is important to understand that the health care industry is in the midst of major transitions that will ultimately affect all of us. Here are some of the changes we can expect over the next decade:

- Fewer physicians in private practice, more employed by hospital systems and large physician groups

- Increased focus on the overall health of the patient and less on isolated episodes of care (e.g., greater attention to follow up after a hospitalization, use of "medical homes" to coordinate care, organization of providers into "accountable care organizations")

- More adoption of health information technology, including health information exchanges to allow secure transmission of health information among health care providers, computerized decision support for physicians, use of information systems to collect quality and utilization data about providers, and expanded use of telemedicine in rural areas

- More attention to patient engagement using secure email, patient portals and electronic personal health records

- More attention to population health (e.g., using statistics from individual providers about how many of their patients receive vaccinations, are under monitoring for control of chronic diseases, etc.)

- More use of advanced practice nurses, pharmacists and other providers to supplement care provided by physicians

These trends will likely mean that while health insurance available to consumers may still vary greatly from state to state, all of us will see major changes in how our health care is provided. This transformation of the health care industry will affect not only plans offered through the health exchanges, but employer-sponsored plans as well.

1. The Affordable Care Act

1.1 What Is the Purpose of the Affordable Care Act?

First, a bit of history. We all know that the biggest percentage of Americans with insurance coverage get it through their jobs. Why is health insurance in the United States tied to employment? In part, this dates back to around World War II, when workers were scarce due to the war effort, but employers were prohibited from competing for workers by offering higher wages. Large employers competed for workers by offering health insurance coverage.

> Why do most Americans get health insurance through their jobs, when that's not typical for other advanced economies? It's history.

Health insurance, like any other kind of insurance, works better if there are a large number of insured individuals who pay premiums to cover the claims of the unfortunate few who incur large losses. So, health insurance worked fairly well for large employers. Because they had thousands of employees of varying ages and health conditions, insurers could offer them good rates. The cost of isolated employees who had large claims (e.g., an employee whose child was born with an expensive health condition) was offset by premiums paid for many healthy workers. The employer-based health insurance system worked less well for smaller employers. A health insurer preparing a quote for a small employer would look closely at the ages and previous health expenses of the employees, to avoid taking a large risk. Small employers with an older or less healthy workforce had difficulty getting coverage at reasonable rates. In many states, insurance commissioners tried to make health insurance more affordable for small employers by adopting rules restricting small group rating practices, but insurers always had the option of leaving the small group market entirely if this made the small group market too risky for them.

Individual insurance coverage was an even less attractive market for health insurers, and so they were very selective in what risks they took (i.e., who they allowed to enroll). Prior to passage of the Affordable Care Act, an individual seeking to buy health insurance outside of an employer group could be denied coverage if he/she had a preexisting condition, or in some cases offered a policy that excluded claims relating to the preexisting condition. Also, an insurer could refuse to renew a policy for someone whose health status deteriorated.

> Problem #1 for American health care: access

All of these market differences created problems, especially when individuals became unemployed or moved from one employer to another. State and federal law tried to address these market problems in various ways. The Consolidated Omnibus Budget Reconciliation Act (COBRA) required employers to offer an employee the right to continue insurance coverage for a time following termination of employment. (However, employees seeking to use COBRA coverage are frequently surprised by the size of the premium since it includes the employer portion that they have not paid in the past.) The Health Insurance Portability and Accountability Act provided that individuals covered by an employer policy for a period of time were given credit for the time they were covered and could more easily move to a new employer plan.

In spite of these measures, the U.S. still had a large number of individuals without insurance coverage. This is the first major problem of our health care industry: access. Lack of health insurance leads to difficulties accessing care. Hospitals are required under federal law to provide emergency care to patients with an emergency medical condition, and in some areas of the country, federally qualified health centers are available to provide primary care, charging a fee based on the patient's income. But this still left many gaps. While anyone can go to a hospital emergency room and get care for an immediate medical emergency, most uninsured people trying to make an appointment with a private physician will not be able to find a doctor to care for them. This is the problem the Affordable Care Act (the ACA) seeks to address.

There is another major problem with the U.S. health care system, and that is the high overall cost of care. The U.S. pays far more for health care than any other nation. This is due to many factors: the overall wealth of the U.S. economy (which means that we simply have more money to spend on health care than less developed economies), the reliance on expensive technology, lack of transparency for consumers seeking information on the cost of care, the high cost of drugs and health care services in the U.S., and lack of coordination and continuity of care. It remains to be seen whether the ACA, and the trends transforming the health care industry overall, will be able to help us deal with this second major problem. This will be a critical challenge for our nation as a whole, and for everybody's individual financial future.

> Problem #2 for American health care: cost

1.2   Basics of the Affordable Care Act

The ACA has two main goals:

- Expansion of health care coverage. This was to be accomplished through making more low-income individuals eligible for Medicaid, and combining several policy features to make insurance coverage available and affordable to individuals and small employers (described in more detail below).

- Bending the cost curve. As mentioned above, the U.S. has the most expensive health care system in the world. There are many reasons for this, but a major factor is that most health care is provided and paid for on a fee-for-service basis. Doctors and hospitals have been paid based on volume of services rather than for improving the health of the population they serve. The ACA contains several tools to change this, such as encouraging the creation of "accountable care organizations" in the Medicare program that are set up to deliver all the health care required for a group of individuals in a coordinated manner.

Medicaid is a health plan for the poor and disabled that is funded jointly by the states and the federal government. The ACA's goal of expanding Medicaid to about 138% of the federal poverty limit hit a major snag with the decision of the U.S. Supreme Court in the constitutional challenge to the ACA. The Court faced a complex case which challenged the constitutionality of the ACA as a whole. In June 2012, the Court upheld the law, but with one major exception. The Court held that the states could not be forced to accept the expansion of Medicaid as the price of continuing to participate in the Medicaid program, and required that individual states be allowed to choose whether or not to expand Medicaid eligibility for their citizens. As of late November 2013, half the states and the District of Columbia will implement the expansion, while in the remaining half Medicaid eligibility rules will remain the same.

Aside from Medicaid, how did the ACA seek to expand the availability of affordable health insurance? Through a combination of tools to make insurance available to more people, hold down the premiums insurers would charge, and provide premium subsidies for individuals who made too much income to qualify for Medicaid, but earned under 400% of the federal poverty level.

1.2.1   The Health Insurance Reform Provisions of the ACA

As one part of the effort to make insurance more available, the ACA established health insurance reform requirements for health insurers, aimed at covering more people for more health conditions in both the employer group market, and the individual market. These include:

- Requiring insurers that offer coverage in the individual or group market in a state to offer all products approved for sale in the state to any individual or employer[1];

- Guaranteed renewal of coverage, except for nonpayment of premium, fraud, and other limited circumstances[2]

- Prohibiting insurers from denying coverage based on preexisting conditions, or limiting or excluding benefits based on the fact that the condition was present before the date of coverage[3];

- Prohibiting discrimination based on health factors (health status, medical condition, claims experience, receipt of health care, medical history, genetic information, evidence of insurability, or disability)[4];

- Requiring health plans to cover a beneficiary's dependents up to age 26[5];

- Prohibiting lifetime or annual limits on benefits for individuals[6];

- Prohibiting rescission of the policy except for fraud or intentional misrepresentation[7];

- Requiring coverage of preventive health services without any cost-sharing requirement (i.e., deductible, coinsurance or copay)[8]; and

- Requiring claims appeal process to meet certain standards[9]. Many states already provide protections for consumers in dealing with denial of claims for services, but the regulations under the ACA set minimum standards for state-mandated appeal processes.

The ACA also restricted the ability of insurance companies to set premiums in the individual or small group markets. Insurers are permitted to vary the premium only with respect to the following factors[10]:

- Whether the plan covers an individual or family;

- The geographic rating area;

- Age, except that the rate may not vary by more than 3:1[11]; and

- Tobacco use (meaning use of tobacco on average four or more times per week.

As an additional tool to hold down insurance premiums, the ACA required insurers to spend a minimum percentage of premium on health claims (the 80% medical loss ratio), and rebate any excess to policyholders.[12]

These restrictions on insurance company practices are usually popular. The other side of the coin, which is not as popular, are the mandates: the requirement that all eligible individuals must have insurance, or pay a tax penalty[13], and the requirement that all employers with 50 or more full-time employees must provide qualified health insurance, or pay a tax penalty. The first is called the "individual mandate", and the second is the employer mandate, frequently called "play or pay".

> People generally like the ACA's restrictions on insurance companies, and dislike the mandates – but the two are connected.

Why is the good stuff and the bad stuff connected? The reason for the mandates is to avoid the premium "death spiral" that could otherwise result if insurers were forced to cover everyone, including people with serious health conditions.

Health insurance, of course, is of the greatest value to those who need it the most: people with chronic health conditions, people at risk for serious illness, etc. Since these people are the most likely to seek to buy health insurance (especially in the individual market), insurers were at risk for "adverse selection" – that is, their policyholders would not reflect the general health of the community, with a mix of healthy and sick people, but would tend to be sicker. In the pre-ACA days, insurers managed their risk by underwriting and plan design. They would not offer policies to people who would be likely to have extensive claims, deny coverage of pre-existing conditions, and charge premiums based on health status. They also sometimes designed plans to appeal specifically to healthy people (e.g., by including fitness benefits). Any insurance company that did not manage its risk of adverse selection could find itself in a death spiral: it would have to keep increasing premiums to cover greater claims, which would make its policies less competitive, which would make its pool of beneficiaries smaller and smaller, which would increase its risk even more.

The ACA attempts to prevent the premium death spiral by guaranteeing to insurers that they will be able to spread claims over a large population. Large employers have always been able to get better deals on health insurance than small employers, because the insurer knew it would be able to spread the expense of a limited number of high-cost individuals over a large population, many of whom would not have large claims. The ACA tries to bring this benefit to the population as a whole.

1.2.2 Essential Health Benefits

Another feature of the ACA is the requirement that all health plans in the individual and small group markets offer a set of essential health benefits. The ACA required that the package of essential health benefits be similar to the benefits covered by a typical large employer group plan.[14] The essential benefits are:

- Ambulatory patient services (that is, services for patients not confined to a hospital, including doctor visits)

- Emergency services

- Hospitalization

- Maternity and newborn care

- Mental health and substance use disorder services, including behavioral health treatment

- Prescription drugs

- Rehabilitation

- Laboratory services

- Preventive and wellness services, and chronic disease management

- Pediatric services, including oral and vision care.[15]

1.2.3 Actuarial Values (Metal Levels)

In addition to covering essential health benefits, the ACA also required that plans offered in the individual and small group markets meet specific actuarial values (AV), according to the percentage of expected health care expenses that the plan will pay. The AV levels are 60% for a bronze plan, 70% for a silver plan, 80% for a gold plan, and 90% for a platinum plan.[16] The use of these "metal" levels is intended to make it easier for consumers and small employers to compare plans.

The actuarial value means the percentage of estimated health care costs that the plan will cover – that is, what you are buying for your premium dollar, as opposed to paying out-of-pocket through deductibles, copayments and coinsurance. So the higher the AV level, the more you will pay through cost-sharing (a bronze level plan, for instance, will have a lower premium and higher deductibles, copayment or coinsurance than a gold level plan).

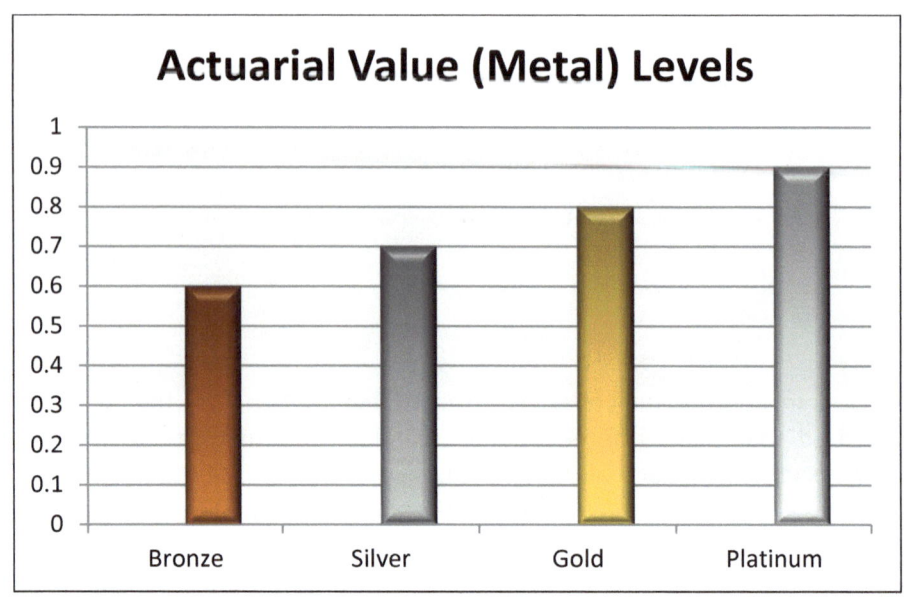

How do these metal levels compare to employer-sponsored plans? A study published in November 2011 of individuals enrolled in the Federal Employees Health Benefits Program Blue Cross/Blue Shield PPO plan found that fewer than 2% were enrolled in plans providing less than 60% of actuarial value, while 36% were enrolled in plans providing 90% of actuarial value (equivalent to platinum plans).[17] Similarly, a study by a leading health benefit consulting firm found that more than 90% of employer plans fell into the silver, gold or platinum levels.[18] The same study found that most large employer plans easily met the premium affordability standard (discussed below). So unless large employers change their health benefit plans in future, people having access to employer-provided health coverage will still be getting a better deal.

1.2.4 Grandfathered Plans

There is a limited exception to the requirement to cover essential health benefits for "grandfathered" plans. A plan qualifies for grandfathered status only if there were no changes in the plan between the enactment of the ACA and 2014. Because insurance plans change frequently, only a small number of plans qualified for the exception.

When this book is being written (December 2013), the requirement that all health plans cover essential benefits has been the topic of considerable controversy. In November 2013, millions of individuals who had been covered by plans not meeting these requirements received cancellation notices from their insurers, who at the time were under a mandate to cease offering more limited plans (other than grandfathered plans) effective January 2014. However, people who were satisfied with their existing plans were greatly displeased with their cancellation. Because of these complaints and the rocky rollout of the federal exchange, the President announced that the insurers could continue offering these plans for an additional year. However, this may not solve the problem for many people, because insurers are not required to continue to offer the plans. An insurer that did want to continue the old plan would still have to get the approval of the state insurance commissioner (usually a time-consuming process). Some state insurance commissioners may not be willing or able to process the insurer's request to continue to offer the plans in time for a January 2014 start.

> The unexpected result of the ACA's essential benefits requirements: cancellation of large numbers of plans in the individual market at the end of 2013.

1.2.5 Model Summary of Benefits

The ACA requires health insurers to describe the basic elements of policies in standardized format. The model summary of benefits and coverage form is available on the Department of Labor website at http://www.dol.gov/ebsa/pdf/SBCtemplate.pdf.

2. Health insurance exchanges

What do you need to know about the insurance exchanges established under the ACA? First, you don't have to buy health insurance through the exchange. If you don't intend to seek assistance in getting coverage, either through the state Medicaid program or through tax subsidies, you can bypass the exchange and go to independent websites that allow you to compare plans, to an insurance broker, or directly to a health insurance company. However, you must get coverage through the exchange in order to get the subsidies provided under the ACA – so if you think you may qualify, check the plans available on the exchange before you look for coverage elsewhere. Second, there is standardization of plans on the exchange, because the plans are organized according to the percentage of actuarially estimated health care costs that the plan covers. The more precious the metal associated with the plans (platinum, gold, silver and bronze), the higher the percentage of costs borne by the plan rather than the individual. So you will see differences in deductibles, copayments and coinsurance among the plans, and there will likely be both HMOs and PPOs from which to choose. (These differences are explained in Chapter 3.)

Why do you have to go through the exchange in order to get the tax subsidies provided under the ACA? The reason is that the exchange serves several functions in confirming the individual's eligibility, by tying in with other federal databases to confirm that the individual is eligible for coverage and has an income level that qualifies for subsidies.

> If you don't plan to apply for Medicaid or for premium subsidies, you can bypass the exchange and buy a policy from the insurer or a broker.

As the exchanges are being implemented, great differences are seen among the states with regard to how affordable the exchange plans are. In large part, this reflects the competitive positions of insurers and health care providers in individual states. Some states, prior to the ACA, were dominated by one or a few insurers, and in these cases the dominant insurer(s) may have little incentive to offer low premiums. Also, among the states and often within a state, there are geographic regions where health care providers have significant market power in comparison with health plans. This has been exacerbated by the recent trend toward mergers and consolidation in hospital systems and large physician groups. In those areas, providers may be able to wield significant market power so that insurers are unable to obtain major rate concessions. Because the insurers in these areas face higher medical costs, they will reflect this in higher premiums.

The ACA also provided funding for the development of Consumer Operated and Oriented Plans (CO-OP plans), which were intended to provide a cost-effective alternative. The co-ops were to be organized on a non-profit basis and to be controlled by their policyholders. Since these participants are new to the insurance market, it remains to be seen whether they will develop as an effective alternative or not.

In addition to differences in premium cost and cost sharing, plans on the exchanges vary with regard to the provider network. The ACA requires that insurers must ensure that the provider network of each plan offered on the exchange meet network adequacy standards (i.e., must have a sufficient number of providers of various types "to assure that all services will be accessible without unreasonable delay."[19] However, as of this writing, there have been complaints both from individuals who are disappointed to find that they cannot access their regular doctor or hospital through exchange plans, and from providers who have not been included in the provider panel.

Both on the exchanges and in the insurance market generally, insurers charge higher premiums for plans with broader networks. This topic is discussed in greater detail in Chapter 3, Section 3.3.

2.1 Who runs the exchange?

When the ACA was enacted, the law assumed that in most cases, each state would run its own exchange. The law provided substantial subsidies for states to cover the extensive administrative costs involved with setting up the exchange. However, because the ACA was so politically polarizing, many states did not want to get involved with running their own exchange. Other states plan to operate a state-based exchange eventually, but were unwilling or unable to do so in 2013 – so for these states, the exchange was operated as a federal-state partnership. As of this writing, 18 states and the District of Columbia are operating their own exchanges, and seven are operating a federal-state partnership exchange in which the state assumes some functions. In the remaining states, the exchange is operated by the federal government.

Some states which are not running their own exchange for individual and family plans are running the exchange for small businesses, known as the SHOP exchange. (This book does not discuss the SHOP exchanges.)

The rollout of the federal exchange website, Healthcare.gov, was plagued with problems. As of December 2013, the front-end problems that originally confronted people trying to sign up for coverage have been eased. Individuals are now able to create an account and shop for plans on the site. However, back-end problems (getting the enrollment details to the insurers who offer plans on the exchange) persist in some cases. This posed a significant problem for anyone wanting coverage to begin January 1, 2014. Even if an individual enrolled by the deadline of December 23, the first premium must be paid in order for coverage to start. On December 18, 2013, America's Health Insurance Plans (the trade association for insurance companies) announced that consumers enrolling by December 23 would have until January 10, 2014 to pay the first premium in order to have coverage retroactive to January 1.

2.2 Who qualifies for coverage?

To be eligible to buy a plan on the exchange, an individual must meet the following criteria:

- The person must be a citizen or national of the United States, or non-citizen who is lawfully present in the U.S.;

- The person must not be incarcerated, other than incarceration pending the disposition of charges; and

- The person lives in the service area of the exchange, and either intends to reside there or has entered the service area with a job commitment or is seeking employment.[20]

If you decide to get health insurance through the exchange, be prepared to provide documentation demonstrating that you meet these criteria. You may need to scan and download documents, such as a passport or driver's license, for this purpose.

2.3 Who qualifies for subsidies?

The ACA provides for tax credits to subsidize insurance premiums, and these are made available in the form of advance credit payments which are reconciled annually with the premium tax credit allowed. The premium tax credits are "refundable", like the earned income tax credit, so they can be used even if the individual has no federal tax liability. A taxpayer can qualify for premium tax credits only if:

- The taxpayer has household income between 100% and 400% of the Federal poverty line for the taxpayer's family size;

- One or more members of the taxpayer's family enrolls in a qualified health plan through the exchange; and

- The taxpayer or family member is not eligible for "minimum essential coverage" from another source.[21]

Premium tax credits will be estimated by the exchange, and will be credited against the individual's insurance premiums throughout the year.

The exchange will calculate estimated tax credits when an individual applies for coverage through the exchange, based on the individual's prior year income. The estimated tax credits will be applied to reduce the individual's monthly premiums throughout the year, and then reconciled to the individual's actual income when tax filings are due for the prior year. If the individual's income has increased or decreased during the year, he/she may have a difference between the estimated premium tax credits and the tax credits that he/she is ultimately entitled to, based on income reported on the tax return. If income has increased and the taxpayer received too much in estimated premium tax credits, he/she will owe an additional tax. On the other hand, if the taxpayer's income decreased, there may be an additional refund.

2.3.1   Household Income in Relation to Federal Poverty Line

The following table shows federal poverty levels (FPL) for all states other than Alaska and Hawaii. Alaska and Hawaii have higher poverty level amounts.

Family Size	100% to 400% of FPL
1	$11,490 - $45,960
2	$15,510 - $62,040
3	$19,530 - $78,120
4	$23,550 - $94,200
5	$27,570 - $110,280
6	$31,590 - $126,360
7	$35,610 - $142,440
8	$39,630 – $158,520

2.3.2   Enrollment in a Qualified Health Plan

To be eligible for the premium tax credit, you <u>must</u> enroll in individual or family coverage through the federal or state exchange. As discussed earlier, this is because the exchanges have the responsibility to verify eligibility for the premium tax credit based on information in federal databases.

2.3.3   Eligibility for Other Minimum Essential Coverage

Subsidies are available only for individuals who are not eligible for "minimum essential coverage" from another source.[22] People who qualify for coverage under Medicare or Medicaid are deemed to have access to minimum essential coverage and therefore, they cannot qualify for subsidies to purchase a plan through the exchange. A person who would be eligible for Medicaid coverage, but does not apply, also may not receive a subsidy. However, if the exchange evaluates the person as being ineligible for Medicaid, that individual can obtain a subsidy.

A person who is eligible for coverage under an employer-sponsored plan is also not eligible for premium tax credits, if the employer plan is "affordable" and "provides minimum value". An employer-sponsored plan provides minimum value if the plan's share of the benefit cost is at least 60 percent (that is, equivalent to a bronze level plan in the exchange). If you are eligible for coverage under a plan sponsored by your employer, you should have received a notice from your employer about whether or not the plan provides minimum value, and whether or not the employer intends the plan to be affordable for most employees. The U.S. Department of Labor's sample form is available at http://www.dol.gov/ebsa/pdf/FLSAwithplans.pdf.

Even if your employer has given you notice that its health plan provides minimum value, you would still be able to enroll in a plan through the exchange and receive premium tax credits if your employer's plan is not affordable for you, based on your income. If the annual premium under your employer's plan exceeds 9.5% of your household income, the plan is not affordable for you.[23] If you decide to get insurance coverage through the exchange rather than enrolling in your employer's plan, you would be able to get subsidized premiums through the premium tax credit.

2.4   How Much Are Premium Assistance Tax Credit Subsidies?

The exchange is responsible for calculating the estimated premium assistance tax credit, based on the cost of the benchmark plan, and the taxpayer's income. The benchmark plan is the secon

d lowest-cost silver plan for the rating area where the taxpayer resides.[24] While the premium assistance calculation is based on a silver plan, you can choose any medal level and the same premium assistance amount will be applied to decrease the premium you will be responsible for paying.

The taxpayer's share of premiums is intended to be affordable based on the taxpayer's income, so the percentage rises as income increases.[25] The following table demonstrates the amount of premium the taxpayer has to pay.

If the taxpayer's income in relation to the federal poverty line is:	Then the percentage of insurance premiums the taxpayer will pay will be:
Less than 133%	2%
At least 133% but less than 150%	Between 3% and 4%
At least 150% but less than 200%	Between 4% and 6.3%
At least 200% but less than 250%	Between 6.3% and 8.05%
At least 250% but less than 300%	Between 8.05% and 9.5%
At least 300% but less than 400%	9.5%

There are tools available to estimate the premium subsidy that you may qualify for, based on income, state of residence and family size. One example is the subsidy calculator provided by the Kaiser Family Foundation, at http://kff.org/interactive/subsidy-calculator/.

2.5 When Can You Enroll in a Plan Through the Exchange?

The exchange is like employer-sponsored coverage in one respect: you can only enroll during an open enrollment period, or if you have a change in circumstances qualifying you for special enrollment. The initial open enrollment period for the exchanges is October 1, 2013 through March 31, 2014.[26] For subsequent years, the annual open enrollment will be October 15 through December 7, with coverage beginning January 1 of the following year.[27]

> You can enroll through the exchange only during open enrollment, or a special enrollment period due to a triggering event.

Outside the open enrollment periods, individuals can enroll in plans through the exchange only within 60 days after a triggering event.[28] Triggering events include:

- Loss of eligibility for minimum essential coverage (e.g., due to a job loss where the individual had coverage through his/her employer);

- The individual gains a dependent or becomes a dependent through marriage, birth, adoption, placement for adoption, or placement in foster care;

- An individual or dependent becomes a citizen, national or alien legally present in the U.S.;

- The individual's original enrollment or non-enrollment was due to error, misrepresentation or inaction of an agent of the exchange; or

- The health plan substantially violated its contract with the enrollee.

2.6   What Insurance Options Will You Find on the Exchange?

If you are eligible to enroll in a qualified health plan through the state or federal exchange, the number of options you will see will depend on your local insurance market. It is up to insurance companies to determine whether they want to offer plans through the exchange in a particular geographic area, and also, insurers must be licensed in the state in order to offer policies there. In some areas, several insurers will offer a variety of plans through the exchange, while in areas where there are one or two dominant insurers, choices will be much more limited. Your overall cost will depend on the medal level you select, running from the least expensive bronze plans through the most expensive platinum plans. In some areas, plans may not be available at all medal levels. Even within a level, you will find differences in premiums, in cost-sharing (deductibles, coinsurance and copayments) and in the provider networks offered. Generally, the more expensive plans will have broader networks.

Sound confusing? The next section of this book will help guide you in making some of these critical choices.

3. Health insurance basics

This section applies not just to health plans purchased through the exchanges, but to any health insurance, including employer-sponsored plans.

3.1   HMOs versus PPOs

Once upon a time, health insurance was provided through indemnity plans: that is, the insurer just paid for medical costs incurred by the beneficiary. However, due to the high cost of American health care, indemnity became an endangered species starting in the 1980's and is now extinct. It was followed by various forms of "managed care".

Health maintenance organizations (HMOs) also have a long history, starting in the 1950's. The theory behind HMOs is that because the health care providers participating in the HMO bear financial risk for the cost of an individual's health care, they will be more likely to provide good preventive care and monitoring so that serious health problems can be prevented, or at least detected sooner so that expensive complications are minimized.

The first HMOs were "staff model" HMOs, which are unified systems of hospitals and employed physicians. Staff model HMOs still exist (Kaiser Permanente is an example). A second model of HMO, the "independent practice association" (IPA) model, became more popular in many parts of the country. In an IPA model HMO, independent physician practices come together to contract with insurance companies, and agree to provide care to the individuals who select the physicians in the IPA as their primary care physicians (PCPs). The IPA bears a substantial part of the financial risk of providing care to the individuals assigned to them. Typically, the insurance company pays the IPA a flat amount per member/per month, called a capitation rate. There often are separate risk pools for expensive types of care, such as hospitalization, and the IPA can earn a bonus if the hospital costs for its patients are less than the amount set aside in the risk pool.

Why should you care how your doctor gets paid? Because having a lot of their pay at risk motivates the IPA to police its member doctors to make sure that most care is provided by members of the IPA, and that costs are kept as low as possible. This means that a lot of rules are put in place that limit your choice of provider. You won't be able to see a specialist unless you get a referral from your PCP. If you go on your own, you won't get reimbursed for any of the cost of non-approved care. Usually, the HMO will provide no coverage at all for providers outside the network. There are exceptions for care that you urgently need when you are traveling outside the HMO's service area, and rare exceptions for highly specialized care that is not available from any network provider. In some areas, HMOs may also offer a hybrid type of plan, which has elements of both HMO and PPO. This is called a "point of service" (POS) plan, so called because the beneficiary makes the choice of staying within the HMO network or going outside at the point of service. POS plans will provide some coverage for out-of-network care, but with a penalty; you might find that 80% of the cost is covered for a network provider, while only 50% is covered for the same service out of network.

In some areas, HMOs are unpopular because of the limitations on the beneficiary's choice of provider. In these areas, preferred provider organizations (PPOs) predominate. A PPO will still have a provider network. The provider network can be very broad, including most providers in the area, or narrow (including fewer physicians and hospitals, sometimes just enough to assure adequate coverage). An insurance company sets up a PPO by contracting with physicians, hospitals and other providers to be participating providers. There are great variations in how the provider gets paid. Frequently, physicians are paid based on a fee schedule. Hospitals can be paid based on a fee schedule (in many cases the Medicare fee schedule, multiplied by a percentage), a per diem rate for each day a beneficiary is in the hospital, or a discount from the hospital's customary charges. In a PPO, the insurance company bears most of the risk of the cost of care.

If you select a PPO, you may be able to see any provider, but the insurance company will pay a higher percentage if you use a network provider. For example, you might have a 20% coinsurance if you are hospitalized at a network hospital, but 50% if you go out of network. In addition, if you use a network provider, you get the benefit of any discount that the insurance company has negotiated. So if a doctor's customary charge for an office visit is $150, but the insurer has negotiated a rate of $100, then you pay $20 and the insurer pays $80. In contrast, if you see an out-of-network physician, you likely will have to pay the entire charge of $150, and the insurer will reimburse you 50% of what it considers to be a "reasonable and customary" charge for the visit. Also, PPOs, just like HMOs, will require preapproval in order to cover certain services, like hospitalization (other than emergencies) and outpatient surgery. Since you pay more for out-of-network services, you could find yourself paying more in a narrow-network PPO plan if you use a lot of out-of-network providers, even if the premium is lower for the narrow network.

> Comparing HMOs and PPOs, you will typically find that the HMO offers lower cost with greater restriction on your choice of provider.

When you compare HMO and PPO plans, typically the HMO will charge lower premiums but impose more restrictions on your choice of provider. Don't base your insurance choice on premiums alone, however. The cost-sharing provisions included in the benefit plan design may have an important effect as well on your total costs for health care and health insurance. In some areas, HMOs have lower cost-sharing than PPO plans.

3.2   Cost-sharing

Cost-sharing is the health insurance industry term for the portion of the cost of care that is borne by the beneficiary. Cost-sharing helps the insurer lower its medical claims expense not only because of the beneficiary's direct contribution, but more importantly because it influences the beneficiary's decision on whether or not to seek care. The theory is that if the beneficiary has to pay a copay each time he sees a doctor, he or she may not go to the doctor for every sniffle, and therefore the insurer won't have to pay for care that turns out not to be medically necessary. However, if copays are too high, this can backfire. An individual could put off going to the doctor until his/her condition is more serious and requires more expensive treatment. There is considerable debate in the health care industry about the level of cost-sharing that causes people to forego medically necessary care. Delay in getting medically necessary care both risks greater illness and impairment for the individual, and greater cost for the insurer if more intensive care is ultimately needed.

Insurers also anticipate that cost-sharing may motivate beneficiaries to be smart shoppers and select more cost-effective health care providers. However, it is frequently difficult for people to get specific information on what a specific provider will charge for a particular service. Lack of price transparency is another major challenge for the health care industry and all of us health care consumers. Many insurers are trying to address this problem by collecting information on comparative costs of their participating providers and displaying this on their websites for use by their beneficiaries.

Annual deductibles, coinsurance and copayments are all forms of cost-sharing. While this book does not discuss it in detail, it is important to recognize that the law now requires parity between mental health services and general medical services in the application of the various kinds of cost-sharing.

> Be sure to make a careful choice between a plan with lower premiums but higher deductibles and copays, and a plan with a higher premium but lower cost-sharing.

How do you choose between a plan with a lower premium but higher cost-sharing, or a higher premium and lower cost-sharing? First, think about how often you need to go to the doctor, how many prescriptions you take, and other health care services that you use. If you use health care services frequently, the higher copayments and coinsurance you will have to pay may exceed the amount you save by paying a lower premium. Second, do you have savings available to pay for a higher deductible, so that you are not prevented from getting care when you need it? If you can readily pay for care on your own until you meet the deductible, it may make sense to select a lower-premium plan. This is especially true if you have access to one of the tax saving plans discussed in Section 4 of this book.

3.2.1 Deductibles

A plan's annual deductible is the amount that the individual must pay out-of-pocket on an annual basis before the plan will begin to pay claims. Annual deductibles can range from zero (rarely) to high amounts, such as $10,000 for catastrophic-type plans. A high-deductible plan can be beneficial for people who do not expect to use many health care services, or for people with substantial savings who can afford to take the risk that they may need to use personal resources to pay for care. There are tax-deferred savings accounts that can be used in combination with high-deductible plans (discussed in Chapter 4).

Deductible example: You visit your primary care doctor. The allowable charges are $175.00. You pay a $20 copay, and the remaining $155.00 is charged against your deductible. You have to pay the $155.00 also, and the plan does not start to pay until you reach your deductible.

3.2.2 Coinsurance

Coinsurance is the percentage of allowed charges that the individual pays for particular services. The allowed charges will depend upon the contract between your insurer and facility. This type of cost-sharing is typically used for hospital care and outpatient surgery. For example, your plan may cover 80% of the cost of an outpatient surgery, meaning that you would be responsible for the remaining 20%. Again, these percentages would apply to the rate that the insurer has negotiated with that provider.

Coinsurance example: You have outpatient surgery. Your plan has a 20% coinsurance requirement for outpatient surgery. The allowable charges are $2,000. You have to pay $400 and the plan pays $1600.

3.2.3 Copayments

A copayment is a set dollar amount that you have to pay for a specific service, such as a doctor visit or a prescription. This can vary based on the type of service or item. For example, you may have a $20 copay to see your primary care provider, and a $50 copay to see a specialist. Some plans use "tiered networks" with different levels of copayment for each tier, to encourage you to see certain providers, based on the insurer's evaluation of the quality, cost-effectiveness or both of the provider.

For prescription drugs, usually there will be a lower copayment for generic drugs than for name brands. This, of course, is to encourage you to use generic drugs when possible. Some insurers also adopt drug formularies. The idea of a formulary is that if there is a class of similar drugs which have the same purpose and similar effects, but different prices, the lower-price drug will be included in the formulary. Then, a lower copay will be charged for formulary drugs than for non-formulary equivalents. Frequently, insurers contract with specialized administrative companies, known as pharmacy benefit managers, to manage prescription drug benefits.

> *Copayment example: You fill a prescription for a generic drug. You have already reached the deductible on your plan. You pay the $10 copayment, and the plan pays the remaining cost of the drug.*

3.2.4 Ceiling on annual or lifetime benefits

As described above, the ACA prohibits caps on annual or lifetime benefits. Therefore, these limits will be encountered only in grandfathered plans (i.e., plans in place before 2010 which have not been modified). For a plan having benefit ceilings, the plan will stop paying claims once the annual or lifetime ceiling is reached.

3.2.5 Out-of-pocket maximums

If a plan has an out-of-pocket maximum, that means that once you have paid the annual deductible, plus coinsurance and copayments sufficient to meet the out-of-pocket maximum, then you will no longer have to pay cost-sharing amounts. The purpose of the out-of-pocket maximum is to protect people who have high medical care needs, such as people suffering from chronic illness or who require many medications, from being unable to afford care.

3.2.6 Coverage Examples

The following examples demonstrate the combination of cost-sharing elements found in many plans. The amounts included are examples only and may not reflect the cost of services in your community.

Having a baby (normal delivery)

Amount owed to providers: $7,540
- **Plan pays** $5,490
- **Patient pays** $2,050

Sample care costs:

Hospital charges (mother)	$2,700
Routine obstetric care	$2,100
Hospital charges (baby)	$900
Anesthesia	$900
Laboratory tests	$500
Prescriptions	$200
Radiology	$200
Vaccines, other preventive	$40
Total	**$7,540**

Patient pays:

Deductibles	$700
Copays	$30
Coinsurance	$1320
Limits or exclusions	$0
Total	**$2,050**

Managing type 2 diabetes
(routine maintenance of a well-controlled condition)

Amount owed to providers: $5,400

■ **Plan pays** $3,520

■ **Patient pays** $1,880

Sample care costs:	
Prescriptions	$2,900
Medical Equipment and Supplies	$1,300
Office Visits and Procedures	$700
Education	$300
Laboratory tests	$100
Vaccines, other preventive	$100
Total	**$5,400**

Patient pays:	
Deductibles	$800
Copays	$500
Coinsurance	$500
Limits or exclusions	$80
Total	**$1,880**

3.3   Provider network

As mentioned earlier, insurance companies contract with a network of physicians, hospitals, pharmacies, ambulatory surgery centers, home care agencies and other health care providers to provide care at an agreed rate. If you select an HMO plan other than a point-of-service (POS plan), you must see a network provider in most cases to have the HMO pay for your care. (There are exceptions for emergency care, and urgently needed services when you are traveling outside the HMO's service area.) PPO plans will cover out-of-network care, but you will have higher out-of-pocket costs for copays and coinsurance.

Both HMOs and PPOs will maintain lists of contracted providers. If you want to get care from a particular physician or hospital, you should check the provider list before signing up for a plan. For physicians, you should also make sure that the physician is accepting new patients. Also, some plans use tiered networks, in which copays are lower for some physicians than for others.

As discussed earlier, there is usually a trade-off between the size of the network and premium charged for the plan. PPOs with large networks will charge a higher premium, and in return you get more choice of network providers. HMOs and narrow network PPOs will charge lower premiums in comparison with large networks. Many of the plans available on the exchanges are narrow-network plans, and because of the cost advantage, narrow networks are becoming favored for employer sponsored coverage as well.

How to choose a health care provider is a complicated matter beyond the scope of this book. While many people depend simply on location or word of mouth in choosing a doctor or hospital, there are now more sources of information on the quality of care provided by individual hospitals, doctors and other providers. Many insurance companies provide quality information on their websites. Consumer reporting services, such as Consumer Reports, Angie's List, and similar services will provide ratings for a fee. There are no-cost on-line comments from sites like Yelp. The Medicare website has extensive quality information available, at http://www.medicare.gov/forms-help-and-resources/find-doctors-hospitals-and-facilities/quality-care-finder.html. The Leapfrog Group, which was originally established by large employers to collect information about patient safety, quality and efficiency of care at hospitals, provides information for consumers at http://www.leapfroggroup.org/cp.

3.4 Covered benefits

As discussed in Section 1.2.2, the ACA requires that all health plans provide the ten essential health benefits. Some plans may also provide additional benefits not required by the ACA. In some cases, state law mandates that insurers offer certain benefits. In other situations, the insurer may believe that the benefits will appeal to consumers. For employer-sponsored coverage, some employers may require that the insurer offer additional benefits, because the employer believes that including some services (such as fitness-related services) will help improve the health and productivity of the workforce.

3.4.1 Exclusions

Most insurance plans will have a description of services that are not covered, even if they fall within one of the general categories of covered services, such as hospital services. It is typical to find exclusions for experimental treatments. Experimental treatments can be defined in various ways, but typically are described as treatments which involve drugs or medical devices that have not received final approval from the Food and Drug Administration, or treatments which are not in accordance with customary standards of medical practice.

Another customary exclusion is for cosmetic procedures. Under this exclusion, plastic surgery done to improve the patient's appearance alone would not be covered, but procedures performed to improve the function of a body part would be considered a covered service. It is also typical to exclude coverage of services provided for the convenience of the patient or health care provider. Nursing home care is also not covered under most health insurance policies.

Probably the most important exclusion is for services that are not medically necessary. The definition of services that are not medically necessary will be specified in the policy, but generally, services are not considered medically necessary if they would not be considered part of standard medical practice, or represent a more intensive level of services than needed for the patient's condition. For example, if an x-ray would be adequate to diagnose a condition such as a suspected fracture, the insurer will not pay for an MRI unless there is a documented need for the more expensive service. If a kind of surgery is customarily performed on an outpatient basis and there is no reason based on the patient's condition that the patient has to be admitted to a hospital, the insurer will only pay for outpatient surgery at a hospital outpatient department or ambulatory surgery center. Similarly, if a patient's condition is stable and he/she can safely be discharged from the hospital, the insurer will not pay for additional hospital days.

In many cases, the insurer will require that the medical necessity of the procedure be reviewed in advance; this is called pre-certification. If the procedure is not authorized in advance, the insurer will not pay for the service unless it was provided on an emergency basis.

3.5 Grievance procedures

Insurance policies will specify a procedure for contesting a denial of coverage by the insurer. In some cases, state law may require a particular process, such as review by an outside physician. If you want to appeal a denial, be careful to get a description of the grievance process and follow any time limits specified. In most cases, you cannot contest a denial through legal process unless you have completed the grievance process provided under your policy.

3.6 Coordination of Benefits and Third Party Liability

If you are covered by more than one health insurance policy, or if you are injured by a third party (e.g., in an auto accident), your policy and/or state law will specify what portion of your health care costs must be paid by the insurer.

4. Special tax benefits to pay health care costs

There are special tax rules that can take some of the sting out of the out-of-pocket costs of deductibles, coinsurance and copayments.[29] While one type, flexible spending accounts (FSAs), are available only through your employer, health savings accounts (HSAs) are not so restricted. If you purchase a plan through the exchange that is HSA-eligible, you can use the HSA to save for out-of-pocket expenses on a tax-favored basis.

While there are some other tax-favored health accounts (such as Medical Savings Accounts and Health Reimbursement Arrangements), FSAs and HSAs are the most typical.

4.1 Flexible spending accounts

Typically, an FSA is set up when you sign a form agreeing that your employer will reduce your salary by a specified amount and put it into the FSA. This essentially allows the FSA contributions to be made on a pre-tax basis, reducing your taxable income. You can use the FSA to pay for eligible medical expenses, including reimbursing yourself for payment of deductibles, copays and coinsurance under your health insurance plan. The amount that can be contributed to the FSA is limited to $2,500 per year.

The main restriction on FSAs is that they are "use it or lose it". While the employer can allow claims to be submitted for a limited period of time after the end of the year, any balance left in the employee's FSA after that period is forfeited.

4.2 Health Savings Accounts

A health savings account is just what it sounds like: a trust account set up to pay health care expenses. The main restriction on HSAs is that they are available only if your health insurance is a high deductible health plan. A high deductible health plan must have a higher annual deductible than typical health plans, and a maximum limit on out-of-pocket expenses (the sum of the annual deductible, plus copays and coinsurance). For 2014, the minimum annual deductible is $1,250 for self-only coverage, and $2,500 for family coverage. The maximum out-of-pocket limit is $6,350 for single coverage and $12,700 for family.

If you are using an HSA arrangement set up by your employer, your contributions to the HSA can be set up on a pre-tax basis, the same as FSA contributions. If you make contributions directly to the HSA account rather than through a salary reduction arrangement with your employer, the contributions are deductible even if you do not itemize deductions. Also, contributions to the HSA account made by your employer are excluded from your taxable income. There is a limit on how much you can contribute to the HSA. For 2014, the maximum contribution is $3,300 for individual coverage and $6,550 for family coverage. People over age 55 can also make a catch-up contribution of $1,000 annually.

Income earned on the HSA account is tax-free, and distributions are tax-free if used for qualified medical expenses. Unlike the FSA, you can retain amounts saved in the HSA from year to year. Also, you own the HSA account, so it is portable if you leave your employment.

5. Health insurance through your employer

There is great variety in the types of plans offered by employers. While there has been much speculation about whether the ACA will encourage more or fewer employers to offer health coverage, we'll have to wait to see the full impact. Recently, some large employers have announced that while they will continue to maintain an employee health plan, they will discontinue coverage for the employee's spouse. Industry experts speculate that employers are taking this action because with the ACA coming into full effect, the spouse would have an option to obtain coverage through the exchange and would not be left without an insurance option. There have also been reports of some employers opting to pay employees a subsidy to purchase insurance through the exchange, rather than establishing or maintaining an employee health benefit plan.

Employers can establish an employer-sponsored health plan in a couple of different ways. The employer can enter into group enrollment agreements with one or more insurance companies, and the companies will then enroll employees and their dependents into their insured plans. In that scenario, the insurer bears the insurance risk for the cost of health care services in exchange for the premium, and the laws of the state where the policy is issued will apply to the plan, including mandated benefits and state requirements for appeal of claims denials.

Employers can also self-insure for employee health costs, and contract with an insurance company to administer the plan. These self-funded plans can be indistinguishable to the employee from a regular insured plan, since typically the employee will still get an enrollment card with an insurance company's name on it. However, self-funded employee health plans are not subject to state insurance laws, and instead are governed by the Employee Retirement Income Security Act (ERISA). For that reason, state mandated benefits will not apply.

A new trend in employee health benefits is the use of private exchanges. This has nothing to do with the exchanges established under the ACA. In a private exchange arrangement, the employer designates the amount of its contribution to employee health benefits, and then the employer selects from a range of insurance options, typically assembled by an insurance broker or benefit consultant. The private exchange idea appeals to some employers, in the same way as many employers favor a 401(k) plan for retirement benefits rather than a traditional pension plan. The employer limits its obligation to the amount it contributes to the plan, and the employee typically has a wider range of choices from which to select.

Conclusion

We hope you found this guide helpful in negotiating the insurance choices available to you. Our health insurance system is extremely complex, and constantly evolving. The ACA is causing insurers that have mainly been focused on serving the large employer market to rethink how they can appeal to individual consumers. Expect to see more variations emerge in future years as the market continues to develop.

About the author

Patricia D. King is a health law attorney practicing in the Chicago area. She has over 30 years of experience representing health care providers and provider-sponsored insurance entities. Pat blogs about consumer issues in the health care industry at www.myhealthcaredollar.com.

Notes

[1] 45 C.F.R. § 147.104.
[2] 45 C.F.R. § 147.106.
[3] 45 C.F.R. § 147.108.
[4] 45 C.F.R. § 147.110.
[5] 45 C.F.R. § 147.120.
[6] 45 C.F.R. § 147.126.
[7] 45 C.F.R. § 147.128.
[8] 45 C.F.R. § 147.130.
[9] 45 C.F.R. § 147.136.
[10] 45 C.F.R. § 147.102.
[11] The insurance industry estimates that this limitation will have a major effect on premiums, because it has been typical in most markets for insurers to use five "age bands" in setting premiums.
[12] 45 C.F.R. § 158.240.
[13] 26 U.S.C. § 5000A.
[14] ACA, Section 1302.
[15] 45 C.F.R. § 156.110.
[16] 45 C.F.R. § 156.140.
[17] ASPE Research Brief, *Actuarial Value and Employer-Sponsored Insurance*, U.S. Dept. of Health and Human Services Office of Health Policy, Nov. 2011.
[18] *What Do PPACA Standards Mean for Employers' Health Plans*, Towers Watson Insider Oct. 2012.
[19] 45 C.F.R. § 156.230(a)(2).
[20] 45 C.F.R. § 155.305(a).
[21] 26 C.F.R. § 1.36B-2.
[22] 26 C.F.R. § 1.36B-2(c).
[23] 26 C.F.R. § 1.36B-2(c)(3)(v).
[24] 26 C.F.R. § 1.36B-3(f).
[25] 26 C.F.R. § 1.36B-3(g).
[26] 45 C.F.R. § 155.410(b).
[27] 45 C.F.R. § 155.410(e).
[28] 45 C.F.R. § 155.420(d).
[29] See IRS Publication No. 969, *Health Savings Accounts and Other Tax-Favored Health Plans*.

www.ingramcontent.com/pod-product-compliance
Lightning Source LLC
Chambersburg PA
CBHW040817200526
45159CB00024B/3018